A Butterfly with Teeth

Kendall Bradley

Copyright © 2018 by Kendall Bradley

All rights reserved.

ISBN 978-1-62806-189-5

Library of Congress Control Number 2018953603

Published by Salt Water Media
29 Broad Street, Suite 104
Berlin, MD 21811
www.saltwatermedia.com

Cover image used via unsplash.com user Elijah O'Donell

for my love Ronda,

who has saved my life

and with great thanks to

Karen, Doug, Karen, and Philip

I ask, not out of sorrow,

but in wonder. - Milosz

Table of Contents

Where Do Poems Come From?   1

Thus   2

Image   3

Upper Bayside, Accomack County   4

After the Fall   5

Piano Jack   6

Seaside Road   8

Stepping Out for Some Fresh Air   11

Evening   12

The Sad Truth   13

How Long Does It Take To Get Things Right?   14

Land of In-Between   15

Star Stuff   16

Maiden's Lament (17th Century)   18

Available Delights   19

Oyster, VA (Three Poems)   20

Reversal   23

This Poem Is   25

Now   26

Early Morning on Parker's Creek	28
New Hospital	29
In His Hands He Holds	31
Because	33
Wheat Field	34
Sniper Assassins	36
Night Storm	39
Panther	40
A Wise Man	44
Lightning Bugs	45
Fire Lovers	47
Riptide	49
Listening	50
Spirit Carver	51
The Marsh at Dusk (For the Children)	52
Such Poetry as This	53
Because I Am Old Enough	54
River of Dreams	55
The Ruins of America	56
A Dying Man	57
Morris	58

Percy's Closet	59
Drought	60
Mystical	62
Most Likely	63
Blue Dot	64
Pirate as Poet	65
Specters	66
Even for This	68
Freedom	69
Dreams of What	70
Please	72
End of Day	73
Only So Much	74
Before You Came Into My Life	75
Not There Yet	76
Let	77
What Is Here That Is Not Here?	78

Where Do Poems Come From?

Heartache and the fear

of doom,

dreams of goldfish,

skies rent by rainbows,

the faint music of the moon's footsteps

on the roof of a deserted house,

a smile stalked by the mortality

of smiles,

the twisted limbs

of lightning torn trees,

the quick wild eyes of small animals,

the inner light of stones

in the kingdom of quarks,

love lost and love gained,

a spider's web

in the mirror of transcendence,

graveyard flowers

enchanted by dew,

a cry in the wind

as night swivels into day.

Thus

Sun and moon,

gravity, frogs,

and gum drops,

voice mail and twitter,

a sprained thumb

and small intrigues...

we take so much

for granted

like getting up

in the morning

and walking

down the stairs.

Image

A bus lurching

and careening

down the darkened

secondary road,

its driver on an undisclosed

mission from God

and blind drunk

on cheap whiskey,

the faces of the passengers

blanched and dumb,

the stark, helpless

anticipation

of personal demise

becoming a palpable

stench.

Upper Bayside, Accomack County

Beyond the ditch banks
just into the woods,
daffodils rise up
through February brambles
beside the tumbled steps
of the time haunted
houses of Messongo
and Marsh Market.

Glassless windows
with broken mullions
look out on back roads
like the dark eyes
of chary backwater girls
that are stuck forever
in sepia photos
from the 1930s.

Soon honeysuckle, wisteria,
and the leaves of sweet gum
will obscure the weathered
clapboard and sagging roofs

as they fade away
into lush springtime
shadows.

After the Fall

Concrete has
an unforgiving,
obdurate character

especially at my age.

Thus I think
as I lay sprawled
on the cold,
unyielding surface
taking careful
inventory
of my pain

perhaps too ready
to ridicule
my clumsiness

but actually,
for this moment
at least,
just being thankful

there seem to be
no broken bones

and knowing that
with a little effort

I will soon be
ambulatory
once again.

Piano Jack

My grandfather

told me about

Piano Jack

how as a young man

he could

work the ivories

like a demon,

making you

go crazy and wild

or set you to crying

with the sheer

magic of his soft

touches.

He told me

how he was good

enough

for Philly

or Baltimore

or anywhere

but he got

into the horses

and he got

into the craps

and his luck

ran out

so they

broke both his hands

so bad

he could

hardly even cull potatoes

or feel up the girls

behind the grader shed

after that.

Seaside Road

- for Dave Harris

On the fringe of the continent

in early March light,

I drive the snaking black road

beside fields of winter

rye and ancient groves

of sycamore, oak

and loblolly pine,

past long lost graves

of masters and slaves,

of potato farmers

and Algonquin braves,

past doublewides and

tottering shacks,

ante-bellum mansions

and turn-of-the-century

farm houses.

From Magotha to Oyster,

Boxtree to Goshen,

Red Bank to Willis Wharf,

I hear the maritime musings

of raw-boned watermen

riding upon the sea wind.

I see the magic seaside loam

stretching to the woods,

the prairie-like marsh beyond

and winding guts leading

to barrier islands

or the dancing blue

of Ramshorn Bay.

It is indeed a good thing,

a sacred wisdom

to save what we can

of this menaced land

and thinking thus,

I think of you,

now retired in Virginia Beach

yet here still,

a presence not

imagined but felt

as I drive along.

We had different professions

but they overlapped,

to my benefit,

taking me time and time again

along the vistas of Seaside Road,

and over swale and slough

to the secret places

few have seen.

I need to thank you

for the gift,

and all that you taught me

along the way

in word and deed

before and after

I even knew

it was happening.

Sorry I did not tell you,

until now.

Stepping Out for Some Fresh Air

Clear winter
night sky,
frost already
on the deck rails.

In the moonlight,
a feral cat
slips beneath the shed
at the edge
of the yard

as a semi runs
through its gears
out on Route 13.

In the sky,
among the glimmer
of Ursa Major
and Cassiopeia,
the blinking lights
of planes head
to Norfolk
from Boston
or New York,

shiny fuselages
filled with their
captive cargo
of tedium and
untold dreams.

Evening

Form is emptiness. Emptiness is form. – The Heart Sutra

Geese are on the wing

over the winter marsh.

They honk and are gone,

heading east.

Near the landing,

a boat motor starts

and then sputters off,

suddenly mute.

At the edge of

a narrow gut near

a small tump of cedars,

I stop the sound

of my own feet

and suddenly

need to know:

who is this

who now listens

so intently

to the silence

of snow?

The Sad Truth

Sometimes it hits us
out of the blue,
unsolicited and undeserved.
like a random body punch
that takes our breath.

It can be as blunt as an iron pipe,
as raw as an open wound,
as subtle as a look
that chills,
as sinister as a smile
that is looking at us
as if from the wrong face -

and there's plenty of it
to go around.

Few of us are willing
to admit to it
openly

but we all do it,
often blaming it on
each other.

How Long Does It Take To Get Things Right?

Of course
it is slow work,
even for
the most
dedicated

but
I think
it is taking
me
much
too long.

I have
to conclude
that

either
I have
no real
talent
for it

or

I am not
trying hard
enough.
Is there
any other
explanation?

Land of In-Between

Strung along the highway

like amber stones

in a necklace for the night,

the lights of

the little clapboard towns

of the Eastern Shore

appear suddenly out

of the rural darkness

then pass quickly

back into the same

greedy blackness,

little more than

electromagnetic whispers

shunting through the windshields

of Jersey bound truckers

and tourists speeding south

toward the boardwalks

of Virginia Beach.

Star Stuff

- for Doug

What are we but

molecular refugees

from singularity

and supernovae

our double helix

of yin and yang

fashioned from

the broken wings

of fallen stars

the dreams

of constellations

ciphered into

our very genomes.

Yet to what end?

Are we

but ghosts

of what has gone before,

or shadows

which foreshadow

what is to come?

Are we the messengers

or the message

that nameless stars

have formed?

Maiden's Lament (17th Century)

Much too soon

you have left

to begin your

journey

beyond the

far mountains

and across

many seas

to strange

and uncertain

lands.

Here

in this spot,

you asked me

to mourn

our parting

with a song

but now,

even

the sweetest notes

of my flute

are cruel

beyond words.

Available Delights

Late May

or early June:

fresh picked asparagus

lightly sautéed

in butter,

fried seaside drum,

local strawberries

in simple syrup

topped with real

whipped cream...

I find myself

taking extra time

to savor fully

these precious

but fleeting

available delights

knowing they come

but once a year

and more years

might not come

at all.

Oyster, VA (Three Poems)

I.

Nine miles east of this tiny hamlet,

as the gull flies, the ocean batters

what is left of Cobb's Island,

inexorably pushing the narrow spit

westerly toward the mainland.

Northern millionaires

once embarked from Oyster slip

to dine on black duck

and sip expensive whiskey

on the veranda

of the island's renowned hotel

before its balustrades

became fancy driftwood

tossed into the marshes

by the great hurricane of 1896.

II.

Before the oysters gave out,

Herman "Hardtimes" Hunt lived

in a ramshackle house

outside of the village

and became its most famous son.

Philosopher, raconteur, rapscallion,

proprietor of the first and only Academy

of Clam Stomping and Oyster Shucking,

he once ran for the State Senate

and then Lieutenant Governor,

knowing full well that

life was too short

not to delight in its salty and

magical fresh shucked

sweetness.

III.

In a low hung cinder block building

hunkered down along the docks

near rusting marine railways

and stacks of crab pots,

an unobtrusive salvation unfolds

as the sanguine future of oysters

moves restlessly in fiberglass vats.

The sterile tripoid spats greedily

feeding on plankton will soon be

on their way to floating upwellers

and then to culches on the salty flats

of The Thorofare or Mockhorn Bay

where they will get fat and juicy

and ready for upscale

East Coast restaurants

and the seedy raw bars

of tourist towns.

Reversal

The earth's poles

have been reversed.

I am looking east

toward the ocean

awaiting tsunami

or tidal wave

but nothing happens.

There is a big screen

TV in the sky.

The screen lights up.

The government

is trying to tell us

something

but the words

blink on and off

in garbled script.

The media

has nothing to say.

The screen goes dark.

It is raining.

The rain

scorches the earth

upon contact

making little fires

everywhere.

In our town,

cats are flying

like birds,

and all the birds

are lying languidly

on back steps

like cat Buddhas

oblivious to the rain's

fire.

Parachutes drop

from the sky.

Under the chutes

are metallic skeletons

with red hibiscus eyes

and they are clutching

baby rats.

Down they come.

This Poem Is

A bare
tree limb
emerging
from fog

this poem is
a wounded
thought
clinging to
a high tension
wire

this poem is
a death
that is
the mother
of beauty

this poem is
gasoline
and a
match

this poem is
a butterfly

with teeth.

Now

- for RPB

The passion

is still here

but comes in

many guises.

It can still shout

and roar

but can also

whisper to our

more subtle delight.

Our once rough edges

have been worn

smooth as river stones

and feel good

to the touch.

Our contentment

with each other

has become strong

as trees with sound roots

reaching deep

toward the center

of the earth.

We don't defy

gravity but embrace it

yet still can dance,

as young lovers do,

high in the air

above the trees.

Early Morning on Parker's Creek

Flat bottomed scow

and an old Evinrude,

winding seaside creek,

narrow but deep enough.

Mallards and pintails take wing

over the still dark marsh

as I chug along,

miles from the nearest

traffic light.

New Hospital

A realtor's sold sign

marks the spot

and the field on which

the new hospital

will be soon be built

is bright green

with winter rye,

so very green

in the late December sun.

As I ride past

the designated site

I think about what

it will be like at first

after the site work

is completed and

the asphalt and curbing laid,

after the masons and the framers

and the roofers

and the drywall hangers

and the tilers

and the equipment technicians

have all done their thing,

after the ribbon cutting

with the smiling faces

of all the board members,

the bankers, and the local politicians,

when the first patients

are wheeled through

the gleaming corridors

or taken to their rooms

on polished gurneys

and that hospital smell

has not yet settled in.

I think about IVs slowly

dripping in new private rooms

and prayers being said

and tears being shed

and who will be

the first to be born

and who will be

the first to die

and who will be the first

to cry out in anguish or pain

within the walls

that are not yet there

in the field of winter rye

so very green

in the late December sun.

In His Hands He Holds...

His undersized hands

are not large enough

to hold the whole wide world,

they are not large enough

to hold America

from sea to shining sea,

they are not large enough

to hold hope for those

who are hungry for hope,

they are not large enough

to hold great dreams

for a country that needs

great dreams

to keep it great.

But his hands

are large enough

to hold hatred,

they are large enough

to hold disdain for hope,

they are large enough

to hold greed,

they are large enough

to hold lies,

they are large enough

to hold a noose for America,

they are large enough

to hold a torch,

not a torch to lead a people

out of darkness,

but a torch to burn things,

a torch to incinerate

dreams.

Because

Because nothing lasts

beauty is possible

because nothing lasts

beauty is pain

because nothing lasts

pain is a possibility

we can move beyond.

Wheat Field

In a grain of wheat

I see clay ovens

baking loaves

formed by primeval

hands.

In a grain of wheat

I see a city of gold

with golden towers

and golden streets

melting in the sun.

In a grain of wheat

I see a beast with

three heads feasting

on human flesh

and drinking

blood from wine skins.

In a grain of wheat

I see lovers,

hesitant and afraid,

reaching for

one another

across a ditch

of fire.

In a grain of wheat

I see hope and despair,

two ravens

sitting on a fence

above a wheat field

as twilight nears.

Sniper Assassins

Words are

sniper assassins,

their laser sights

are trained on egalitarians

and Sumo wrestlers,

on politicians and

girl scouts.

The eyes of words

are dark as

black holes

and they are

watching

every move

we make,

waiting to suck

us into their

verbal vortexes.

Their mouths

are stuffed

with magic air

and whistling

winds.

They can bring

tornadoes

and the riot

of devastation

out of empty

parking lots

into the trailer parks

of our minds.

There is no shelter

from this,

for to exist

is to suffer

their consequences.

Words

can save us

or bring us

to ruin

but they don't care

one way

or the other.

To expect something

of their promises

is foolhardy or worse.

Perhaps we need

to send out

bounty hunters

and bring these

desperados to justice

vigilante style

but the problem is:

the ropes we swing

from the hanging trees

could be for us.

Night Storm

Shadows taunt

the howling trees

until the moon

is wrecked

on shoals of cloud,

its cargo of light

spilling into

the daunting deep.

As the wind tears

dreams dissolve.

As the wind rips

our moorings loosen.

This will be a long

and sleepless night.

Panther

- for Karen

The dreams came

as all dreams do,

unbidden.

I was five or six

and knew I could not

predict or prepare

only accept the fearful

uncanniness

of this particular

recurring terror

as I walked alone

in some unfamiliar

shadow terrain,

always that,

and the sudden

almost subtle shift

of dreamscape

that let me know

I was being stalked.

In spite of myself,

I would turn

and see you,

as I knew I would,

sleek and silent,

in the far distance

watching me,

now coming after me

and closing fast –

always that.

Blacker and quicker

than fear itself,

you would be upon me

in a heartbeat,

halting before me,

with your ancient

yellow eyes

and fangs

of instant death,

powerful haunches

preparing to pounce…

and then I would wake,

always I would wake

trembling and uncertain

whether you were

now in the room,

or down the hall,

or in the yard

among the trees,

waiting for me...

How many times

did you come for me

and how many times

would I breathlessly

save myself

before I found

I could bear this horror

no longer and

in one defining moment

of dream grace

I turned to face you

and unexpectedly found

kind eyes staring

at me,

slowly reached out

my hand

and you did not pounce

but instead

let me stroke your head,

then took me

upon your back

and leaped into the night,

the stars and moon

flying by

and my hair wild

in the wind

for what seemed

like hours...

As I look back

over the years,

I realize, my totem,

my friend,

how very great

your precious gift was

and yet how

very dear

the price also,

since I would never

dream of you

again.

A Wise Man

He always said

that true wisdom

is knowing that

nothing really

matters

while pretending

that everything

matters indeed.

He said

it was very important

to pretend so well

that you fool

even yourself.

Lightning Bugs

Called fireflies

north of the Mason-Dixon line,

we tend to use

the more dramatic appellation

and we wait

from autumn to late spring

for the enchanting

cold fire ritual

of silent bioluminescent

mating calls

to begin anew.

I think of childhood summers

and the mason jars

with perforated lids

which made an almost

mystical sporadic light

in hot upstairs bedrooms

and how the bugs

would be dead by morning

if we didn't relent

and shake them

out the window

before drifting off to sleep.

I try not to think

of one summer night,

some years later,

as I sat nearly drunk

on the sagging front porch

of a house that no longer stands,

when the bugs were so thick

along the dark line of trees

at the wood's edge

that they seemed to me

like the dream time replay of

muzzle flash in a hot LZ

as once described to me

by a fellow collector

of lightning bugs

who didn't make it back

from his second tour

of Nam.

Fire Lovers

> Arson is almost as good as Prozac – Joe Hill, *The Fireman*

The treacherous,

unforgiving,

moon dappled,

black shadowed,

twisting and sorrowful

midnight back roads

of Accomack County

call out to the

would be lovers:

ride me, ride me

without shame or regret

and show the world

your crazy unfulfilled love,

present the fragrance

of smoking wood

upon the alter

of love,

send the roaring orange

orgasmic flames

into the open arms

of the lonely night.

Do this

and the wild thrill

of your secret deeds

will be your

fiery passion

that will burn

and burn

and burn.

Riptide

Be careful,

it can pull even

strong swimmers

down and out.

When it happens,

the lucky ones

make it back in

just getting shell burned

or body slammed

by the surf

while the unlucky ones

are swept

all the way out,

shark bait heading toward

the Gulf Stream.

Listening

Racing

down the street

in front of our house,

two pocket rockets

splinter the night

into jagged pieces

and then speed on

to other roads.

I listen

as crickets and cicadas

and a nearby barn owl

slowly put the pieces

back together

and back yard

earth worms

return

to their dark

and silent

dreams.

Spirit Carver

- for Coop

Sometimes,

perhaps it is enough

just to be

able to discern

the ancient

and enchanting

language

in the feel

of the wood,

in the smell

of the wood,

in the wondrous

shape the wood

has been given

by wise hands

which know

the ways of spirit

and the speech

of trees.

The Marsh at Dusk (For the Children)

Beware the pompey
on the prowl
before the coming
of the night.

With seaweed hair
and bull shark teeth
he moves through
the marsh on silent
webbed feet.

His claws are
bleached bones
strong as steel
and his heart
throbs a bloody
tidal beat.

Taller than a man
and quicker than an eel,
he is coming for you.

His osprey eyes
can see tiny movements
far away
even in the dimming light

as he seeks
his evening meat.

Such Poetry as This

Li Po
embracing the reflection
of the full moon
in the Yangzte-

Hart Crane
leaping from the stern
of the *Orizaba*
into the Gulf of Mexico-

Sylvia Plath,
head in the oven
in her London flat,
gas turned up
a little higher
than the last time-

tragedies all...

but what meter, what rhyme,
what words, gentle or grand,
though written on the page
with living human blood,

could give us
such poetry as this?

Because I Am Old Enough

Because I am old enough
for my wants not to hurt me,
I will tell you what they are:

I want to walk with you
hand in hand
on the first beach
in the beginning of time.

I want to steal
a sapphire from the moon
and place it glittering
in your hair.

I want to lie with you
in night's sweet darkness,
our bodies merged as one
for all the ages of the earth.

And when
the last dawn begins
to brighten the last sky
I will ever see,
I want to drown myself
in the infinite ocean
of your eyes.

River of Dreams

Stars float face down
in the torpid river of dreams,
and the moon has been
snagged by the bony grasp
of the resentful dead.
It appears on the verge
of strangulation
while dark insects swarm
its pallid flotsam mask,
whirring in an incandescence
of buzz...

I stand as if tethered
to the precarious bank.

I could be the hero who frees the moon,
carrying it gently into the woods
and nursing it to health before
releasing it to glide once more
safely in the sky high above the river
of dreams.

But I hesitate, I prevaricate,
I do not enter the water.

I am afraid of the stars,
of what their faces may reveal
if rotated upward by my wake.

The Ruins of America

On an interstate

leading to a major city,

someone had erected

a sign which read

WELCOME TO THE RUINS

OF AMERICA.

It wasn't long before

that sign was taken down

and hauled away.

A new, much larger sign

was put in its place

and surrounded

by a tall chain link fence

topped with three strands

of barbed wire.

This sign read

AMERICA, LAND OF THE FREE

and no one came

to tear it down.

A Dying Man

Some might say
magic is
infinite space
folding in on itself
until it bursts open
like a gigantic
birthday piñata

covering the earth
in rose petals
and dandelions -

or magic is a dream
walking sideways
like a sand crab
that suddenly turns
into a silver gull
of wild imagining.

For me,
magic is taking
enough breaths
to stay alive
one more night

so I can
open my eyes
and see you
in the glory of daylight
once again.

Morris

> *the voices said "do things, break things,*
> *tear things, destroy things" – Morris Odell Mason*

Half man and half child,
he was the self-proclaimed
"killer for the Eastern Shore."

One night in 1978,
after two bottles of TJ Swann,
the demons called
and Morris answered.
He beat Miss Maggie
with an ax handle,
nailed her to
her living room chair
and burned
her house down.

From the shadows
he watched the flames
for a while before moving
down the railroad tracks
to another town
and other deeds.

Seven years later,
oblivious to the candlelight vigil
outside the penitentiary walls,
an unrepentant Morris requested
for his last meal
two Big Macs and a Coke.

Percy's Closet

Deep in the woods
off Bradford's Neck Road
the ghostly dresses
were lovingly hung
in the moonlight
on wires spread
from bough to bough,
and they would flutter
in the breeze
like gossamer dreams.

From this ethereal
wardrobe Percy chose
the cotton dresses
he wore to the Wachapreague
carnival each July,
where for one ticket he
could ride and ride and ride
on the merry-go-round,

beguiled by the music,
and the lights,
and the french-fries,

and the giggling,
gesturing children.

Drought

All day, every day

beneath a yellow sky

the fields do a slow burn

and every day

the people start their day

with the insidious taste

of dust

in their coffee and cereal.

At night,

they have begun

to dream of swollen

black clouds

and the smell of rain

on hot asphalt.

They dream of the sound

of lawnmowers choking off

on lush grass

and of rainbows

in the late afternoon.

They dream

that there is a God,

that he is a watery

and not a dusty God,

that he is a God of tall corn

and garden hoses,

that he is a caring God

who will deign

to answer

the plaintive prayers

of parched souls.

Mystical

You and I
stepping out
on the porch

into early October,

bare feet
on the cool wood,
harvest moon
over our neighbor's
roof,

the incense smell
of wood smoke from
down the street.

At times like this
the best thing is:

no more
words,

just

be.

Most Likely

Most likely
it will be on a day
that begins
like any other,

a normal day
characterized
by its nondescript
features
like coffee or tea,
its muted
expectations
of sunshine or rain.

When it happens,
it most likely
will be something
unforeseen,
unanticipated,
something seemingly
capricious

that will rise up
in surreal majesty
to grab the day
by the throat

and rip it to pieces.

Blue Dot

We call it home,

this Copernican spec,

this blue dot

galactic outpost,

this minor warp

in space/time,

this inconsequential orb

unobtrusively spinning

like a forgotten top

on a dusty shelf

of the universe's

lost and found

department.

What better place

for us to preen and strut

like ironic barnyard cocks,

claiming dominion

and seeking glory

oblivious

to the sharpened ax

leaning against

the fence.

Pirate as Poet

Rum soaked rhymes
spin pillage tales
of blackest hearts
and blacker deeds,
of plunder won
and glory seized
from feckless foes
on bloody seas,
of maidens ravaged
on leeward shores,
of rigging hung
with sun-bleached skulls,
of fearsome planks
and sharkish swales...

And so it goes,
and so it goes,
'til ships are stove
and bones grow old
and the sea wind calls
without reply,
for the deeds are done
and the rhymes are run
and longish nights
in rum free rooms
bring forth the pain
of phantom limbs,
and remembered hymns
to watery tombs.

Specters

This big house is crowded

with a throng of 68 visitors,

each year of my life has

ex nihilo assumed a persona

and become an uninvited guest

and I the reluctant host.

They are everywhere: in the johns,

in the hallways, in the living room,

in the bedrooms, in the kitchen,

spilling out onto the porch,

young and old and middle aged.

Some are bashful, retiring,

standing in the corners like wallflowers,

others assume a raucous mien

jostling for attention,

arguing among themselves

on points of pride

and issues of importance,

some are looking at me

with unsettling recrimination.

Some I know better than others,

and some I barely recognize,

some I remember much differently,

than they now appear,

some I can welcome warmly

but others I disdain and fear.

These are the scoundrels

and vagrants and ingrates

to whom I give a wide berth

on my way back

to the liquor cabinet.

Even For This

I.
In the slow motion
of forsaken time,
in darkness
and a forlorn wind,
a backwater creek
is being dragged for corpses,
the hard-eyed boatmen
are peering at
the search-lit water,
the onlookers are standing
at the edge of the marsh
like wounded herons
in the cold shadows.

II.
It is a cruel dawn
that offers no solace
from a merciless night
and a cruel day
that follows.

Yet,
we are made
even for this,

even for this.

Freedom

It takes a harsh

and bitter wisdom

to know that

we are never truly free

and that when we

make our escape

from our own particular

captivity,

it is only from one prison

to another

we jauntily go,

no matter how pleasant

the new accommodations

at first may seem.

Dreams of What

While too many of us
have no dreams at all,
that is a different matter
of deep concern.

Those of us, however,
who do dare to dream
should be forewarned that
dreams can be dangerous.

Too many of us
become indentured to our dreams
and never break free
from their grasping bonds,
their mirrored subterfuge.

Perhaps it is because
our dreams are often
manufactured for us
and the warranties expire
right before the built-in
obsolescence kicks in.

Perhaps it is because

we so easily lose our way

in a dark morass

of unrealistic expectations

and self-deception.

It is not easy

to find the dream sweet spot,

the dream with heart

the dream we know

feels good and right

the dream that will guide us

not to the mountain top,

but to where

we may need to go.

Please

Please,
I beg the universe,
just let me
do what
I need to do
in my own way
and in my own
time.

You can try to do
anything you want,
replies the universe,
not that I care,

but, regarding
your own way,
it is best
not to focus
too greatly upon it.

Regarding time,
we all hope
to have plenty.

It is best,
however,
not to have
too much,

but just
enough,

not that I care.

End of Day

The day lies face down

on the sidewalk,

a dark stain of blood

oozing toward the curb.

Bystanders gather

as a siren wails.

There is no pulse,

someone says.

Undetected,

the night limps by,

an old miscreant

from the borderlands.

He has

the eyes of a lizard

and a curious smile

and he moves

without haste

toward the heart

of the city.

Only So Much

We can take a lot

and give a lot

but only so much

before we take

too much

and lose it all

or we give so much

we begin to take

without really

knowing it.

Before You Came Into My Life

Before you came

into my life,

I had almost

gotten to the point

where stars

were just stars,

wind was just wind,

and early September

light had become

like any other light.

No one danced

in my dreams

anymore

and there was

no singing

to wake me

from my own

empty silences.

This is how it was

before you

came into my life.

Not There Yet

All my life I've heard
"You're not there yet."

or "Just keep trying,
you'll get there soon."

or "It will all
make sense
once you get there."

After many years
of trying,
I must confess

I'm still
not there yet.

What is worse,
I don't even know
what "there" is

much less where it is

or how I would
even know
if I finally got
there.

Let

Let joy be

a sun-bedazzled tree

in a forest

of somber looking trees

let sorrow be

a burning tree

consumed to ash

to set a spirit free

let hope be

a climbing tree

from which to see

beyond the trees.

What Is Here That Is Not Here?

- for Travis

Everything

and

nothing.

About the Author

Kendall Bradley is a native of the Eastern Shore of Virginia. He holds BA and MA degrees from the University of Virginia where he first began to write verse. This his second book of poems. His first, *Backwater Moon*, was published in 2009.